A Little Book of Rinses

Hair, Body, & Foot Rinses For

Better Health & Energy

Patsy Stanley

Copyright © 2023. Use of any part of this book without permission from the author, their representatives or agents is prohibited by law. All Rights reserved. No part of this book may be reproduced, transferred, modified, or used in part in any way and in any form without the express written consent of the author, agents or representatives.

ISBN 978-0-9991615-2-4

LCCN 2023923400

Disclaimer:

The content in this book is published for informational purposes only, and is in no way intended to be a substitute for medical advice. If you choose to use any of this information, you do so by your own choice. All information included in this book is in no way intended to be used as a medical guide. If you have specific skin problems or ailments on your scalp or physical body, they need to be taken into consideration by you and /or your physician before using any of the recipes or treatments in this book.

This book is dedicated to Heather, the Pisces I searched for in the Moon and found.

Psssttt !! Ear wax is a natural antibiotic.

Some of the content

A Little Bit About Herbs
Two Hair Rinses for the Changing Seasons
Nettle Hair Rinses
Dandruff Control
Foot Baths
Body Rinses
The Fabulous Cucumber
Two Methods Of Making An Herbal Body Wrap At Home
Spinach Body Wrap
Seeds And Sprouts
How To Use Soap Differently
Shampoos
Witch Hazel
Happy Rinses To You
    White Champagne Body Rinse
    Pink Champagne Body Rinse
    Ginger Ale Body Rinse
Granny's Oatmeal Facial
    Granny's 1st. recipe
    Granny's 2nd. recipe
Natural Rose Water Hand Cream
More Body RInses
    White Rose Petal Body RInse
    Yellow Rose petal Body Rinse
Pink Rose Petal Body Rinse
    Red Rose Petal Body Rinse
Other Odd And Ends
    Salt And Eggplant Tooth paste
    Port As A Mouth Rinse
When Not To Wear Perfumes or Aftershave

In the Beginning, there was water...

Most of this planet is covered by water. Most of us is water.

At death, we cry. At birth there is water. The chemistry of tears makes the crossing into each new emotional place smoother and easier.

When we shed tears, we are releasing the chemicals necessary to make the change into a new way of being we shall occupy.

This book is about ways we can honor how we use the water that is both inside ourselves and outside of ourselves. By water, I mean fluids. Some of the recipes given are for mundane, daily use. Others are rituals for sacred, ceremonial use.

The methods and rituals and recipes that were chosen for this book were picked to encourage and expand the thinking about both mundane and sacred water rituals and the powerful places they hold in your personal life on all levels.

Moving water rituals into a more expressive, joyful and honoring place in life gives a person more health, vitality, and humor. Then a zest for life and the curiosity it brings, develops. Then you can run along your path.

Bathing Rituals are Rituals of Purification

The Physical Body After An Emotional Release:

After an emotional process, your physical body has to deal with the break up of the energy block you released through crying, anger, whatever emotions you used. All energy blocks are toxic. The older they are, the more toxic. Because they contain the essence of old, unreleased experiences that were most likely negative.

Also, your body deals with the general toxins you release every day. Adding the extra toxicity of a released energy block to it, can make your body go on overload, which can make it feel pretty bad.

After an emotional release, help your physical body to clear out the extra toxins. Take Baking soda baths, take more vitamin C, get more rest, and drink lots of clean water. These are a few of the basic ways that will help your system clear the toxins out quicker.

Give yourself time to integrate the information and new awareness from the release, before you tackle something new. And the physical body needs time--it has to deal with the released toxins from the energy block, and move them on through itself. Who knows how long that will take?

You must give yourself time to assimilate the emotional release you did, or you will most likely recreate it again! There are lessons to be learned from every release, and that takes time.

To keep growing consciously, and not stay on overload, pay attention to and take care of your physical body after every emotional process, and remember to not push yourself into more processes. Let them come up naturally.

Baking Soda Baths:
Your first few baths, esp. the first one, pulls the early baby toxins out of the skin, so the water may turn gray!
1 box baking soda in a tub of very warm water. Soak for 10- 20 minutes. Rinse off with clean warm water. Get out and rest.

This bath is designed to pull the residue of old toxins out of the skin layers that have been there since birth to six month old.

Your body releases toxins during strong emotional processes.
Depending on the intensity, how old the process is, and the length of the process, you will need to de-toxify, to help get the negative toxin release to leave your system as gently and quickly as possible.

If you become lethargic, headachy, or your feelings may become magnified all over again, it means you are probably reprocessing the old toxins.

What to do about those old memory toxins that you got let go of, and released into the body's elimination systems?
Learn what the elimination systems are and how they work. That information is available online at any time.

There are different ways to release.
A few are:
Making sounds
Colonics
Baths
Sweating
Talking
Walking
Drink lots of water- fluids
Many more

Use common sense. Don't over do.
Because you are a human being, and have to clean up from the physical aspect of life.
When you begin to have movement in the physical body, you begin to support that movement in your other bodies.

Keep your friends for support, don't use them as therapists, or you will eventually do "transference" `with them, and lose them as friends. Utilize therapists for the professional tools that they provide. Keep good boundaries.

Baking Soda or Salt Baths:

Sea salt is best- do after an intense emotional experience –release

Don't stay immersed for over 15 min- 20 minutes because more toxins will begin to release from your body. You've got enough toxins released from the emotional process you just went through. That's more than enough to deal with right now.
Layers of skin and the intestines hold toxins from infancy forward.
They will begin to be released in this bath. Bath water may turn gray or black from these old toxins.

Native Americans use this sweating process – sweat lodge- cleansing technique in conjunction with the cleansing of the soul.

Bubble baths- creates a feeling of safety because each bubble is a tiny shield. Recreates a safe mothers womb-

Laying on mother earth helps reconnect us to our life.

Frozen in fear? Track yourself. Be crafty. Tell what you know. Your name, the planet you live on, the country, the state ,the city, the street address-eventually track yourself, find yourself, go back in yourself.

Powdered mustard- for cleaning energy in hospital settings- Entities don't like it- meaning surgical instruments, meaning sharp edges-
That shine- it takes moon power or silver, shiny, reflective edges to get attention of entities, so

you can request them to leave. Crystals that are flat like mirrors are most effective.

A Little Bit About Herbs

Fresh herbs are best gathered in the morning before the dew leaves them and when they are in their first flowering. The life is most strong in them then. Wash them gently in a strainer and dry them. They can be spread out on a screen or loosely tied together and hung upside down. They like hot shade or the sun to dry in. If you don't have those, then you can put the herbs between dry layers of brown paper bags or hang upside down inside of a paper bag to dry.
The usage ratio of fresh herbs is 3 to 1. Use 3 times the amount of fresh herbs as powdered or dried herbs in your recipes.

Two Hair Rinses For The Seasons:

Red Cider Vinegar Rinse:

The seasons change four times a year all over the world. Each season carries psychic changes in with it. When each season comes in, it is good to use a hair rinse to clear the energy around the head. It helps ease the ability to change your mind so that you can better adapt to the new incoming season and the new psychic messages each season brings with it.
For this purpose, use a thin vinegar rinse. Use red cider vinegar for white is too harsh for the purpose.

Mix 1 cup of red cider vinegar into a quart of tepid to warm water. This will be your next to final rinse water. Mix it in thoroughly, then when you have shampooed and rinsed your hair with water, pour the prepared rinse over your head and hair. Let the rinse stay on a couple minutes, then rinse your hair a final time with clean water.

Always make your final rinse water clean by using a water filter or spring water. Even distilled water is better to use than the tap water we have these days. When you are done, your hair will be restored to its natural acidic balance.

Store any extra rinse in a clean shampoo bottle or squeeze dispenser bottle. It will last for several weeks when stored in a cool place.

If you like using the red cider vinegar rinse and want to use it more often, you can add any of the following herbs to the above recipe. They can all be prepared in the same way.

Steep each herb in 1 cup of very hot water for a few minutes, then let cool. Use a tea strainer, sieve or cloth to strain the herbs from the water. Then add the herb water to the vinegar rinse.

Sage - enhances dark hair- about a half of a cup
Chamomile -enhances light hair - a good palmful
Rosemary - brightens the hair of anyone - 2 good stems
Red Clover - freshens dull hair and makes it smell wonderful. Brings back the happy outdoor childhood memories to the hair. - 1 cup

Dandelion flowers and greens- brings youth and fatness back to the hair---- use 1/2 cup
Other herbs that you like may be used in the red vinegar rinse. Just follow the recipe for the rinse as usual, adding the herbs you like instead of the ones on the list.

Nettle Hair Rinses

Use 1 cup of fresh leaves to 1 quart water, high simmer for several hours, cool, strain, then use as a conditioner or for dandruff.

The following conditioners nourish the hair after shampooing

Open a beer. Add 3 drops of regular, not light, olive oil to the beer. Mix, and apply to your hair. Rinse out after 5 minutes or so.

Apply mayonnaise to your hair and leave it on for 2-3 minutes. Rinse the mayo out with cool to warm water.

Dandruff Control

boil in a covered pan the following, 1/4 cup mint leaves, 1/4 cup red cider vinegar, 1 cup water. Cool, strain, apply to scalp.

To encourage your hair to grow, make a strong tea from hemp products and apply to your scalp.

If you are a blond or your hair has gone to white, it is good to give it a little help by refreshing it with a lemon rinse. Use a real lemon, that way you know it has the natural strength left in it. Take the juice from a regular size lemon and mix it into I quart of water. Rinse your hair with the mixture and let it stay on for 3 minutes.

Then finish with a final clean water rinse. If your hair is white, it will start to clean the dirty yellow look from it after about 6 uses. For the blondes who use color, you won't have to use those chemicals as often.
Rubbing a lemon straight onto the yellowing ends of white hair will whiten the ends. Let the lemon juice stay on for 5 to 10 minutes before you rinse the ends off with clean water.

Red cider vinegar and lemon juice rinses have distinct smells. They clean away the old thoughts and accumulated emotional and memory residue from your hair without it having to be cut.

Beware!
If you have any kind of fungus, do not use vinegar rinses.

Cleaning the energy around the head up with these simple rinses helps the third eye with its cleansing, too. The front of the forehead contains a psychic area that is associated with our ability to smell. The ability to smell is a yang activity. Smells connect us instantly with certain of our memories.

Both vinegar and lemon juice rinses clear away the accumulated memories of smells that are not basic to our memory banks. The smell of vinegar is yin and associated with mother and her smells. How she smelled when she held you when you were a baby and a child, the smells of milk and food and anything you took in are an integral part of the primitive, basic memories of all of us.

The collective sounds that were around when you took anything in during your development helped form the way you view the world with your physical eyes. So the physical eyes work with the third eye to access your memories.

The vinegar rinse helps strip away the old sweetness that isn't needed any more, and allows for the new sweetness to come in. Sweetness being the way we deal with nostalgia, longings, yearnings, and the way we view attachments.

The lemon rinse is much more yang. It helps strip away the old thoughts that have collected in the energy around the head. It cleans and energizes the thought process.

Many people have thoughts in their energy sphere that don't belong to them. They have picked them up and are carrying them around. Clearing the mental energy in this simple way allows a person to begin to recognize their own thoughts instead of someone else's.

Using these rinses at the turn of every season only takes a few minutes and the cumulative benefits are great.

FOOT BATHS:

Raw White Potato Foot Bath

A foot bath made from raw potatoes is a restorative for the feet. It cleans up the feet in a way that soap can't do. Water is a restorative for the earth and for our feet. When you add the raw potatoes, you are grounding in the earth element plus the water element. Slice up peeled, fresh, raw white potatoes into room temperature water. Don't use red or yellow potatoes because they are not acidic enough. Put your feet in the potato water as soon as you have it ready. Read the paper or whatever you want to do while you sit there for about 20 minutes. By that time, the potatoes drawing action will have finished.

Rinse your feet in clean water and dry them off with a rough terry towel if you have one.
A raw potato foot bath is good for those who have athlete's feet or any kind of foot fungus that is trying to start. Try to wear natural fiber socks on your feet if you can. The synthetic ones lessen the circulation and energy going to the feet, making one feel ungrounded and causing many foot problems to begin. You can use this foot bath once a month or at least several times in the summer when the feet naturally sweat the most.

Tomato Foot Bath:

Do you have a problem with smelly feet? Our feet exude a lot. They sweat more than most any other part of our body. They get rid of a lot of toxins from our body.

Go down to the store and buy 4 to 6 cans of one pound cans of crushed red tomatoes. Fresh tomatoes these days don't often have the high acidic content needed, although you can use them if you have them on hand. Use a pan that is stainless steel or made of something that will not draw the tomatoes energy. Tomatoes like to be in metal containers, but if you don't have one, use a heavy plastic container.

Open the cans of tomatoes and pour them into the container and rest your feet in them for up to a half an hour or more. Then rinse your feet thoroughly with clean water and dry them. Leave your socks and shoes off for a while.

A tomato foot bath pulls out old memories of the dark places our feet have walked in. The times when our feet were on guard or ready for flight. Sometimes smelly feet are developed as a defense against other people getting too close to us when we are needing to rest and have private space to ourselves.

Alka Seltzer Foot Bath:

Drop a dozen Alka Seltzers into the warm foot bath. Their fizz works well in a foot bath for tired feet. Use a dozen for fun and less if you're serious, to 1 gallon of water to still get the job done of refreshing the feet. Rinse and relax.

Rose Foot baths

All roses have a heat in them that works with the circulation to free it up, to give it vitality, to thaw it out.

Rose Petal Foot Bath:

Roses are a circulatory restorative when used in a foot bath. Roses draw the heat, the warmth of love down into the feet. They calm the feet down and make them warm again. Helps poor circulation.
(Roses run a contest when they are around heat- they will become hotter than the water they are in.) They exude a magnetic heat. (Esp. red roses)

Pour hot water, not boiling, into your foot bath. Dry roses and make them into a powder. Add one half cup of powdered red roses to the very warm water and stir it up. Let the rose water steep until the temperature of the foot bath is just comfortable enough for your feet to tolerate.
Put your feet in the foot bath and let them warm back up. Soon your feet will feel the Earth's circulation again. The Earth's rhythm will bring

life back to and improve the circulation of your feet, making them want to dance on the Earth once again.

Red rose oil will not work for this foot bath. If you don't have powdered red roses, red rose petals can be used, but you will need at least 2 cups of them crushed down compactly before your put them in your foot bath. Use red rose petals only, for other colors of roses do different things.

Oatmeal Foot Bath:

This foot bath is for people with dry feet. Maybe the heels are rough or hard and the skin is dry on the toes or all over. Or the person is developing the beginning of bunions or corns. This foot bath will soften the feet and moisturize them.

Place 1 quart of very warm water in your foot bath. Add 1 quart of warm cooked oatmeal to the water and stir it up. Place your feet in the bath and think about getting new shoes, or spend the time identifying the hard thoughts you are thinking and how to erase them. Maybe the path you are walking is too harsh, and needs to be softened a little and you can think about ways to do that.

The oatmeal still works when it is cool, so you can stay in as long as you want to. It works at any temperature.

Body Rinses:

Water Lily Rinse To Restore Spiritual Connection

The water lily rinse is a ceremonial remedy for people who take lots of drugs–prescription or non-prescription-a drug is still a drug-on a daily basis for an illness or condition, or for those who have taken hallucinogens, and for those who have had their 3rd eye blown open or it stays open from prescription or non-prescription drug use. The body doesn't know the difference between the two.

This is a more difficult remedy to put together and do, but well worth the trouble because it begins the restructuring of the path the spiritual self needs, to re-connect it back to the physical self.

This is a remedy for too much yang energy that has caused separation to occur in the higher chakras.

This remedy is Ceremonial because it gives Spirit a form-structure to begin to come back into when the paths it usually pours through have been damaged, destroyed, or stay open too wide all the time.

We are all self organizing, and this ceremonial rinse allows for the self organizing process to begin to take place in the exact place where the chaos of the lost path is located, and reorganize it.

Regular medications can't get there. They are pushed off on other paths. The energies have to use a blanket effect.

This remedy goes to the intersection where the connection to the Spirit Ancestors got broken through drug use and works to reconnect it again.

This remedy is best when the flowers are fresh, but that is not always possible. Find a water place that has lily pads and collect the pink, white or purple pointed water lilies growing on top of the lily pads when they are in bloom.

Separate the petals and spread them out to dry on a screen. Spread any other flower parts out to dry also. Do not use a dryer of any kind. Keep the drying water lilies in a spot that has good air circulation. When the water lily petals are dried, place all the parts of each flower in a cotton cloth bag. Then you can place all of the bags into a bigger one for storage. **These particular precious plants work with the clearing of the third eye and the crown chakra**.

They bring back the memories of our spiritual past and reorganize it when it has been lost to us. They grow in water and point up to the universe.

They are a high vibration plant that connects us to our spiritual sources so that communication can continue in that realm of our awareness. This is a relief to those who think that they have lost themselves forever.

Works with the color purple.

Have a container that you will use only for this foot bath. Have the person being treated set down in a chair if possible. If not, the bath can be used in the best possible of circumstances you can create.

Pour 3 quarts of tepid to warm water into your container. Gently add the contents of 3 water lily flowers to it from the bags. Swish them into the water with your fingers and let it set for 20 minutes. Stir gently with your hand 3 times before the time is up. This bath is very specific because it works with restoring forgotten ceremonies that have been lost to the person. This bath must be given to another, you cannot do it for yourself, so be particular who does this for you, if it is to be effective.

The person's feet are placed in the foot bath. The person attending them uses their hands to constantly pour the water back over the person's calves so that it runs back down into the bath container, again and again. This process goes on for 4 minutes.
Then the person getting the bath sits very still for 2 more minutes with their feet in the water. Then the person gets out of the foot bath and goes to the shower. The person giving the treatment pours the lily foot bath water over their head slowly in a stream while they are in the shower. Then the person rinses off with clear water in the shower and goes to rest. Stretches out their legs and feet.

If the person receiving the bath is bedridden or in a wheelchair, then add a small natural sponge to your container and swab their temples with the lily water after you are done with their feet and the calves of their legs.

This is a potent bath that works on many levels to promote healing. It may be used every two months, or 3-6 times a year, depending on the severity of the need.

Soon you will see a new light in the person's eyes and they will have, with your help, done a ritual of reconnection that addresses the needs of their Spirit.

The person giving this bath should dress up and think good thoughts while giving the bath. Give the bath with dignity and not in haste. It was no accident that impressionist artists were fascinated with water lilies!

Watercress Body Rinse:

To 3 quarts of tepid water, add 3/4 cup of powdered watercress. Swish in circles and let steep for 10 minutes. If you want to use fresh watercress, steep 3 bunches of it in hot water for 10 minutes then strain. Add water to make 3 quarts.

Carry your container to the bath tub or shower. Stand in the shower or tub and use a cup to pour the watercress rinse over your abdomen and the lower half of your body. When you are down to the last 2 cups, pour the water over your shoulders and all of your body. Not over your head. Rinse off with lots of clean water right away and towel dry.

The watercress rinse pulls parasitic energies away from the auric energies that we carry outside of ourselves. The watercress rinse cleanses our auric system and strengthens our external defenses from energy leaks so that the processes going on inside of us can stay in their natural process, as they are not interfered with so much after this rinse.

The Fabulous Cucumber:

Cucumbers belong to the Goddess, the Moon. They bring incandescence to matter. The cucumber is at the top of the hierarchy in it's place in the plant kingdoms.

Dried powdered cucumber packed in little cotton hand bags can be used for many things. To cool the temper of a child. When held by women, connection back to their Goddess roots pours in to help them.
Cucumbers are a demulcent, cooling whatever it encounters and gentling the pace.

When anyone is seeing too much, such as in a migraine or A.D.D. conditions, eating a small amount of cucumber 3 times a week will begin to regulate the condition. Pace it, slow it down, cool it off.

Place cooling slices of peeled cucumber on the eye lids when you are reclining. This is a receptive yin position that relaxes the eyes. When your eyes are relaxed, your hearing automatically becomes more acute.

Eyes work with yang energy. They go out and collect information. Hearing works with yin energy. It is receptive. If you really want to hear something, or receive the voice of wisdom for something you are searching to know, then do this when you are in a quiet place.

Fresh cucumber is a facial food. It may be used on your arms and hands, also. Peel and whiz a cucumber or 2 in a blender until they are mushy. Mix briefly so that the cucumber doesn't get warm. You can leave the seeds in them. Always peel away the outer skin before using the cucumber. Peeling takes away the bitterness from the cucumber and leaves it mild and cool with its own moon sweetness.

Mix the blended cucumber with 1/2 cup or more of warmed whole milk or cream. Apply to your face and neck and elsewhere. Leave on until mixture starts to dry, 10 minutes or up to a half hour or so. Rinse off with lots of clean water.

Cucumber powder may be made by peeling fresh cucumbers and slicing them in thin, length wise slices. Lay them on a screen to dry in a cool place that has good air flow. Do not dry them in the sun as the sun will cause them to lose their potency.

When the cucumbers are dried, grind them up in a blender and store the powder in a plain wood container or a dark glass container.

Mix 2 tablespoons of powdered cucumber to a warmed half cup of whole milk for a soothing facial.

Cucumbers are good for bringing down fear. Eat them or hold them.

Two Methods Of Making An Herbal Body Wrap At Home:

The First Method

You can use any size bed, but a twin size bed or massage table is easier to work with when making a body wrap at home. Some people use the little fold away, light weight canvas portable sleeping beds that campers often take with them. When they are done, they just fold them up and tuck them away until the next time.

You will need 2 sheets, one for the bottom and one for the top. Wash the sheets in hot or boiling water to remove other people's energies and to clear any negative energies from the sheets.

You will need 2 pieces of large plastic. Place a plastic mattress cover or a large sheet of plastic over the mattress. While the sheets are cooling, the body wrap herb mixture is applied to the person.
When the bottom sheet is cool enough to handle, place it over the plastic.
Have the person lie down on the mattress and cover them with the top sheet. Wrap the 2 sheets around them and then wrap blankets around them. To keep the heat in, wrap the second sheet of plastic around the blankets.

The person can go to sleep or you can stay with them and talk or play soft music for them.

If they get too warm, then take the plastic off. Stay in the wrap for half an hour, then come out and be massaged or take a shower.

The Second Method

Use the first method, but boil the two sheets in a strong tea water. Use the tea of your choice. The sheets will be the herbal wrap instead of anything else. Wrap the person in the sheets when the sheets are cool enough to handle. Cover them with the blankets and then the plastic sheet. Proceed as in the first method.

Spinach Body Wrap

A spinach wrap is so good for the whole body. It feeds all the parts of it. To make a spinach wrap, chop enough fresh spinach to make 4-6 full cups after it is cooked. What you don't use can be refrigerated in a glass container and reused. Just reheat it in a pan on the stove, not in the microwave.

Add a sparse amount of water to the pan and cook the spinach down on medium low heat until it is limp, about 5 minutes or a little less. Leave the water and spinach in the pan. Let them cool down until they are a little bit warmer than room temperature.

Pour in the blender and whip briefly or leave as is. Mix in one or two cups or more of real mayonnaise, depending on the texture you want the spinach wrap to be.

Now you are ready to apply it. Slather it on, and don't forget to put it on your hair also. Leave your spinach wrap on 15-30 minutes, then rinse it off with lots of clean water. Depending on the thickness of the mixture you made, you may want to shower with a thin soap solution.

Your hair will have a sheen to it and your body will feel fed. The rest can be stored in the refrigerator. It will last a week or so. Use it for facials or for the other parts of your body.

Other herbs or vegetables may be used in place of spinach. You will have to play with the ratios of amounts to get it the way you want it.

Some addition suggestions:
kelp
cooked broccoli
wilted green bean leaves
cooked sugar peas in the pod
cooked dandelion greens
(all are pureed in the blender)

Seeds And Sprouts

Seeds and sprouts are a fine way to get the benefit internally that a rinse provides for externally. They bring the benefits of the spring season and the water element into your body. Everything comes from the seed and it's shell. Be refreshed, renew yourself by giving your body seeds and sprouts.

Sasparilla Rinse For Men

For the men who are feeling impotent and old. Brew up some good, strong sasparilla tea and pour it into a pan. Save a little back to drink.
Rest your hands in the pan, allowing the tea time to interact with your energy. Then pour the tea over yourself in the shower. Wait a few minutes before rinsing it off.

Sasparilla tea is a spring tonic that has been used by people for centuries. It has a sweet, light smell and is rejuvenating to the young man residing in the older man.
Sasparilla tea brings back the vitality through stimulation of the memories of vitality. It brings back the zest from hidden, forgotten places.

Eating pumpkin seeds helps with this problem in men. Sasparilla and pumpkin seeds carry male hormones and the memories of how they connect in a yin manner.
Gensing is helpful as it is yang and carries the memories of ancient male expression.

How to Use Soaps Differently

Some people are not bothered by the soap products sold today, but many others are reactive to them. They suffer from dry skin and the ailments that come from dry skin. They may suffer from chronic skin conditions that are directly related to the soap products they are using.

Most of the commercial soaps we use today are sold to us in too concentrated a form. Many of them are detergents, not soaps.

The liquid soaps and soap jels are too strong for many people in the concentrated method used in packaging them commercially today. When we apply them directly to our skins, we are using them full strength, and our skin may be suffering from them.
The skin is the largest organ we have. It has built in natural cleansing techniques and systems for exuding toxins and breathing.
 These natural systems don't work as well as they could and can when we overwhelm them with a concentrated soap or cleanser.

After awhile of using full strength cleansers, the skin may be getting the message that it is not doing enough or not doing its natural job correctly. When that happens, the skin may react by breaking out or shutting down to a degree.

Since we left the agricultural way of life and went into industry, the move away from familiar scents has been growing, replaced by the idea that we can never be clean enough.

The larger part of the population is living in cities, which forces them to be close together for long periods of time with many people that are not their relatives or cultures in most cases.

The fact that we exude through sweat and other natural body functions and that those functions have always been a part of mankind and keep us healthy, has had to be set aside under the new conditions we have imposed on ourselves.

This is not a new stage of development we are going through in the western world. Europe went through it long before America became a country.

In Europe, as a result of the move away from farm lands into the cities over the centuries, people learned new manners that enabled them to be in large crowds in small spaces. A whole set of new social circumstances came into play. What it means to have good manners and to practice politeness, changed rapidly.

People had to learn new methods as well as new manners to deal with each other. One of the earliest and longest lasting methods developed in order to not offend another person was the use of herbs and perfumes to mask personal scents.
The daily and exotic use of perfumes became a standard for the middle and upper class in Europe and to not participate in the ritual use of them was considered the height of bad manners.

Over time, the illnesses and plagues that were common in those days finally brought the people's awareness of the need to bathe to the surface as they began to get the connection between personal cleanliness and good health.

Before then, it was usual to bathe once or twice a year and to mask their body smells with perfumes. Purification rituals were not the norm. The only Sacred Purification ritual available was Baptism.

When the people realized that the illnesses they were suffering from had something to do with keeping their body bathed, they moved into taking baths once a month. The more daring souls bathed once a week.

Today there are more people on the planet than ever before, and the number is growing. Cities are getting bigger and bigger. People are using deodorants and perfumes more than ever so that the people around them will not smell their personal scents.

Foods are changing from all natural and in season, and that has made an important change in personal body smells. The industrial smells in the cities permeate the air the people breathe and cling to the skin and hair.

This and other factors contribute to changes in each person's own natural smells. Good manners dictate today that we never let another person smell our sweat or our feet or any of our other personal smells.
Once again, as was done in Europe for centuries, we believe that only the lower class of people are rude enough to not hide their smells.

As happened in Europe, this belief has brought on a deluge of overuse of deodorants, scented soaps and perfumes, and scented foods.

The idea has been masked that we are human animals, and that it is a part of our makeup, just as it is for all other plants and animals on Earth, to be able to smell each other. This draws us further away from the inner animal nature that kept us safe. As human animals, we now view each other in a separated way.
We are at risk of losing the ability to understand and assist each other in a primal way.

The reasons for the natural ability to exude smells and to smell them in nature and on other people are myriad and complex. One of them is that smelling someone in their natural state gives us information about the state of their health. Another is that we intuitively know from someone's smell whether to be afraid of them or not.

Ancient cultures, including the Mayan Indians, believed that sweat was a holy distillation from the body of humankind. They collected it in containers and used it in their holy ceremonies.

Soaps:

It is good to be polite. But achieving a balance between our own personal nature and its growth needs requires taking a middle line these days. The following are some ways to accomplish that goal with more ease.

Whatever kind of soap you use to bath your skin with, probably should be diluted. You can buy beautiful bottles and containers for a low price almost anywhere.

If you dilute your soaps using a standard measure of 1/3 soap to 2/3 distilled water, you will find that your skin will be much more able to protect you from infections, rashes and other ailments. Not only that, you will save money and have beautiful containers around the house. And you will still be able to smell you!

To dilute hand soaps takes more work than the liquid soaps that are out now. Hand soaps have to be shaved and remelted and remixed. You might want to keep them on hand for special occasion use.

The easiest way to move from the application of industrial strength soaps is to switch to liquid soaps as they dilute readily. The nice thing about doing this is that you will accomplish smelling "good" and still have your sense of smell at least somewhat intact.

Our sense of smell has everything to do with the development of our intuition. And intuition cannot evolve without being able to smell the natural smells of people and the things around us so that we can categorize them in our systems.

Using biodegradable soaps and shampoos is a safety net. Since they won't hurt the environment, they probably won't hurt you either! Unscented is best, though in all of these.

Shampoos:

Statistics say that more and more people are experiencing hair loss. The most popular theory is that hair loss is due to stress.
I'm sure that is mostly true, and contributing to the problem is that the shampoos on the market today are too strong and are playing a large part in the rising statistics of hair loss and scalp disorders in both men and women.

In case this is a possibility, along with diluting your body soaps, dilute your shampoos until they are thinned down to a texture that can be applied with a squeeze bottle. Take your time and adjust the ratio until you feel comfortable with it.

If you use a small bottle with a tip on it to apply your shampoo, it will make it easier for you. If you take the time to convert to this method, you will obtain the benefits of healthier hair and saving money and having beautiful containers in your bath area that are most welcoming.

When you wash your hair and your body, make sure all areas of it are thoroughly wet before you apply soap or shampoo. Take the time to let the hair follicles and the pores of your skin get ready to work with the soap and shampoo. Let them open and prepare. Let your skin and hair circulate the natural energy that it carries.

Wear Natural clothing as often as you can. Look for 100 % cotton or another natural fiber to at least sleep in. Wear them more if you can. Because synthetic fibers cause the natural flow of circulation of the body's energies to change or be cut off.

Make times outs when you don't wear the perfumes or deodorants. Do this so your body can rest and exude correctly. Find a place of balance where you can still smell and look and dress acceptably to others and still have your natural ways. Be your own natural self as much as you can.

With a little attention from you, before long, you will have your new balanced system in place and your body will thank you!

Witch Hazel:

Witch Hazel is an astringent. It dries the skin out, and has been used for centuries as a cleanser for too oily conditions of the skin.

Witch hazel is also considered to be an eminent protector for those times when you are going to be dealing with "oily" folks. Pour some on a clean white handkerchief or on a white square of cotton cloth and wave it outward in a complete clockwise circle around you before you go to meet with them. Wave your handkerchief as though you were shooing the "oiliness" away.

Here are Happy Rinses for You!

White Champagne Body Rinse:

After you have worn a lot of deodorant and/or perfumes, and you have clinched the deal, and you have gotten what you wanted after a lot of work in the boardroom or office, wherever, when the time of release comes, the sigh of relief that you made it, you won, then the physical body releases. It lets go of the negative buildup you have stored. This is the time to use this special rinse.

It is time for a celebratory rinse!

Use at least 2 bottles of champagne to do this celebratory rinse. This rinse will brisk you up. It will fizz away the old. It will make your mental energy cleaner and more open to celebration.

The mind, the mental body, the brain, likes this rinse.

Choose a champagne that is bubbly. The more bubbly, the better. It does not have to expensive. Open the bottles. Stand in the shower. Pour the bubbly into your sipping glass and the rest over your body. Champagne has a mild, astringent like effect. Rinse off and keep celebrating.

Pink Champagne Body Rinse

Pink champagne poured over yourself in the shower has a warmer effect and gives you rose colored glasses for a while. It could last for several hours. Use this rinse to celebrate a love victory. Rinse off with clean water.

Ginger Ale Body Rinse

A ginger ale rinse gives you an ancient sparkle. It makes you feel wise. It brings the light of the soul to the surface. Open several cans of room temperature ginger ale. Pour it over yourself from the shoulders down. Dance a little, laugh a little, realize how wise you are, then rinse off. **This rinse is most effective when done at sunset.**

Granny's Oatmeal Facial:

Granny's 1st. Recipe:

Whiz 1 scant cup of old fashioned natural oats in the blender into powder. Put the oatmeal in a pan on the stove. Add 2 cups of water to it and cook for 10 minutes. Adjust water amount as needed. Set off burner and cool. Apply when tepid to face, elbows and hands. Rinse with warm water. This facial mixture may be stored in the refrigerator and used for the next few days.
Wrinkles leave. The face gets fed.

Granny's 2nd. Recipe:
Mix as above to make a medium thick paste and apply to the elbows and hands and feet. Rinse with nice warm water. Then laugh.

Here is how to make Natural Rose Water Hand Cream:
Pour 1 cup of distilled, boiling water over 3 heaping tablespoons of dried or powdered rose petals. If you are using fresh rose petals, you will need 2/3 cup of them pressed down. Steep, covered , for 20 minutes. When the rose water is cool, strain and add equal parts of water and glycerin to make the hand cream.
If the rose water is not strong enough and the scent doesn't come through, then you might want to let it steep for up to 3 days before adding the glycerine.

You can adjust the amount of the powdered or fresh rose petals as you make new batches of the hand cream. If you want a different hand cream, you may want to replace the rose petals with mint or another mild herb in the recipe.

More Body Rinses:

White Rose Petal Body Rinse:

The following rinses are for pouring over the body only, not over the head and hair.

To make a white rose petal body rinse, use 2 cups of lightly pressed down white rose petals. Place them in a pan and pour 1 quart of very warm water over them. Cover and let steep for 20 minutes. Strain the white rose petals out. Go to the shower when you are ready and pour the rinse over yourself. Rinse again in clear water, no soap- and dry off.
These rinses are doing their job. The energy is there, working for you, though it may be subtle.

If you are using powdered white rose petals, add 3 heaping tablespoons of them to the quart of very warm water. Then proceed as in the recipe for the fresh rose petals given above.
This rinse will clear your auric field of all but the best intentions that you have. It raises your vibrations and encourages others to see that you are acting on your best intentions, that your motives are pure.

This is a good rinse to do before preparing for a ceremonial event such as marriage.

Yellow Rose Petal Body Rinse:

To make a yellow rose body rinse, you will need 3 cups of lightly pressed down fresh yellow rose petals. If you are using powdered roses, then you will need 3 heaping tablespoons of yellow rose petals. For either one that you use, steep for 20 minutes in 1 and 1/2 quarts of warm water, not hot. Do not cover.
Strain the rose petals out. Go to the shower when you are ready and pour the rinse over yourself. Rinse again with clear, clean water and dry off.
A yellow rose body rinse soothes the solar plexus and brings back the mental sparkle of humor, enthusiasm, and amusement to love. You can see the child in yourself and them again. It helps you expand your fun in life to express and include more. It makes you more light hearted. You might want to dance or sing again.

Pink Rose Petal Body Rinse

To make a pink rose petal body rinse, you will need 1 and 1/2 cups of lightly pressed down pink rose petals. Place them in a pan and pour 3 cups of warm, not hot, water over them. Cover and let steep for 13 minutes or so.

Strain the pink rose petals from the water and discard them. When you are ready, go to the shower and pour the rinse over yourself. Rinse again with clear water and dry off.

A pink rose petal body rinse soothes grief and promotes love and understanding and acceptance in the aura, in the energy field around us.

Red Rose Petal Body Rinse:

To make a red rose petal body rinse, you will need 1 cup of lightly pressed down rose petals or 1 heaping tablespoon of red rose powder. Place the powder or petals in a bowl or pan. Pour 1 quart of water over them. And stir with your hand until mixed. Let mixture steep, covered, for 10 minutes. Strain petals out and discard. Go to the shower when you are ready, and pour the red rose petal rinse over your body. Rinse with clean water and dry off.

This rinse helps with connection to another and gives you warmth and courage. It allows your courage to be accessible to you. It is stimulating and helps you find the words to make any situation you are confronting, softer and easier.

All of these recipes work for both women and men!!

Other Odds And Ends

Salt and Eggplant Toothpaste:

Powdered eggplant is a remedy for many gum diseases. Peel and cube the eggplant and wrap in foil. Bake in a hot oven. If it turns white, it is overdone.
Mash and mix half and half with sea salt and store in a glass container for a toothpaste. Use gently once every week or 2.

Port As A Mouth Rinse:

A dark, rich port wine may be used temporarily as a mouth wash to soothe toothache and to draw out infections. Using this mouth rinse several times a month tones the gums and mouth and helps them to be more healthy.

Boiled Potato Water:

After the potatoes are boiled, there are a lot of nutrients left in the cooking water. Plan to use the water in the rest of your cooking in gravies or something, because it contains so many of the nutrients from the potatoes.

Vegetable water:
Spinach water or any other kind of water from boiled vegetables contains a high degree of nutrients. Use these waters instead of plain water for soups and gravies and for boiling other foods. They can be poured into a pitcher and saved in the refrigerator for up to three days until you are ready to use them in cooking.

If you are not going to use the vegetable water in cooking, then you can feed the water to your plants or something in your yard. They will love it.

When Not To Wear Perfumes and After Shaves Or Colognes

Be nice to other people. Try to remember that many people are allergic to perfumes and to aftershaves and colognes.

Not to mention the people who have asthma attacks when around these products. **Do not wear perfumes on airline flights!! You are closed in, and there is no place for it to go! Don't let your vanity hurt someone!**

If a person has an allergic reaction to perfume or after shave or colognes on an airplane, it might be severe. And there is no where to go, and possibly, no one to deal with it. You just might kill somebody off!

Do not wear any scents into the woods and forests. Pests love them and will flock to you, especially bees.

Some scents irritate and anger animals and flying pests. This is because you are giving off an unnatural scent and they cannot read your intentions through the natural scents you would normally exude. They don't know if you are there to harm them or not.

If you use a weekly body rinse, you will soon find that you smell good all the time and won't have to use perfumes and so forth very often. Another plus is that your energy field becomes toned.

Bathing Rituals: Are Rituals of Purification

Bathing rituals have been a part of humankind's life since the beginning. The Pagan cultures, including the Celtic and Northern European cultures enjoyed and appreciated the way their bodies smelled. They enjoyed bathing and had many rituals around the bathing process. They developed many mythologies and stories about bathing that became rituals of purification.

Many Goddess rituals have their roots in bathing rituals. Bathing purified themselves, which makes the body's energy vibrations higher- and more toned. Bathing gave them strength to start anew. Bathing can be both holy and mundane.

Standing under a waterfall, stepping into a pool or stream, standing under a sprinkler, or getting in your shower gives you a place to be that connects you with the Earth and all of the other people on it. The water rituals we do are meaningful, natural, and holy.

Water carries a deeper meaning for us. Water is associated with beginnings. It is associated with our birth and death processes. Our physical birth is accompanied by water. Before our birth, we lived in a special water. Whenever there is a dry birth, the chemistry of tears is present to help balance the water element.

Tomatoes And Potatoes:
People who eat night shades can get arthritic conditions if they haven't crossed over into the fall of their life successfully. Check with someone to see what vegetables are night shades, besides tomatoes and potatoes. Bones and stones.

A bit of Ginger root is good for the stomach

Men can eat spices easier than women for spices are yang like men are.

Severe colic & multiple ear infections- probably is - check for fungal overgrowth in intestines

Deficient-mental & physical- brain dysfunction possible-get neurological evaluations to know

Rhythmic training is a musical & martial arts discipline

Bittersweet root is used as the magical plant when winter ends and spring starts. Bittersweet evokes the chemistry associated with nostalgia. Sprinkle it on the ground near a tree. Sit under the tree and wait until the chemistry works.

You will have tears from the different parts of you that cry. Spring is this lifetime's emotions.

But bittersweet forever remembers the mothers and the fathers, that's what bittersweet is for.

www.ingramcontent.com/pod-product-compliance
Lightning Source LLC
Chambersburg PA
CBHW070441010526
44118CB00014B/2144